LAIKA:

THE 1ST DOG IN SPACE

Written by Joeming Dunn • Illustrated by Ben Dunn

FAMOUS FIRSTS: ANIMALS MAKING HISTORY

Making 1957 History

magic wagon

Written by Joeming Dunn
Illustrated by Ben Dunn
Colored by Robby Bevard
Lettered by Doug Dlin
Edited by Stephanie Hedlund and Rochelle Baltzer
Interior layout and design by Antarctic Press
Cover art by Brian Denham
Cover design by Neil Klinepier

Library of Congress Cataloging-in-Publication Data

Dunn, Joeming W.
  Laika : the 1st dog in space / written by Joeming Dunn ; illustrated by Ben Dunn.
    p. cm. -- (Famous firsts. Animals making history)
  Includes index.
  ISBN 978-1-61641-641-6
 1. Laika (Dog)--Juvenile literature. 2. Animal space flight--Juvenile literature. 3. Dogs as laboratory animals--Juvenile literature. 4. Astronautics--Soviet Union--History--20th century. 5. Famous animals--Soviet Union. I. Dunn, Ben, ill. II. Title.
  TL793.D86 2012
  636.7'0886--dc22
                           2011011364

TABLE OF CONTENTS

Humans have always been interested in the universe.

Early people praised and worshipped the sun and the moon. Some believed this would give them special powers.

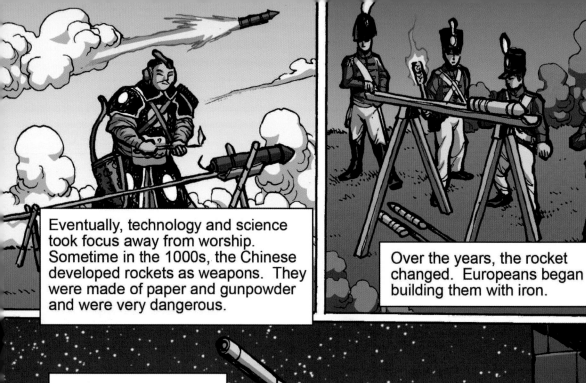

Eventually, technology and science took focus away from worship. Sometime in the 1000s, the Chinese developed rockets as weapons. They were made of paper and gunpowder and were very dangerous.

Over the years, the rocket changed. Europeans began building them with iron.

As time went by, scientists began to see relationships between the objects in the sky.

Johannes Kepler discovered the laws of planetary motion. Sir Isaac Newton explained the laws of motion and gravity.

WITH THE ADVANCEMENTS IN SCIENCE, PEOPLE STARTED TO DREAM OF GOING INTO SPACE.

JULES VERNE AND OTHER AUTHORS BEGAN TO WRITE ADVENTURES THAT TOOK MAN TO THE MOON.

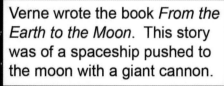

Verne wrote the book *From the Earth to the Moon*. This story was of a spaceship pushed to the moon with a giant cannon.

H.G. Wells wrote about space travelers and Martian invaders. His most famous story of this kind was *The War of the Worlds*.

The idea of space travel had been around for some time. But, Russian scientist Konstantin Tsiolkovsky was the first to design a rocket that could actually go into space.

Tsiolkovsky determined the speed it would take to escape Earth's gravity.

Then, he suggested an engine that could reach that speed.

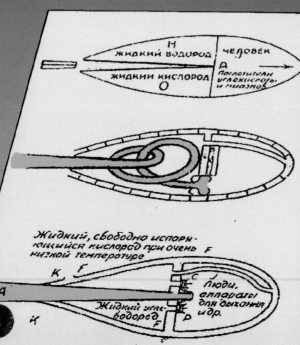

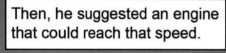

Tsiolkovsky also believed that the correct fuel needed to be created. This fuel would need to have a chemical added to help it burn.

8

Tsiolkovsky next came up with the idea of a multi-stage rocket, or rocket train.

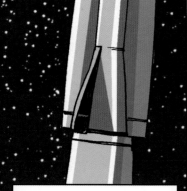

The first stage would create the first push into the atmosphere.

When the fuel was gone, that stage of the rocket would be released to remove weight. Then the lighter second stage would ignite and push the rocket into space.

Other scientists, including Robert Goddard, also started experimenting with rockets.

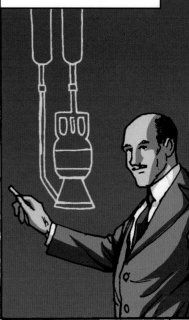

Goddard developed a way to separate and then combine the parts of liquid fuel to be used in the rocket engine.

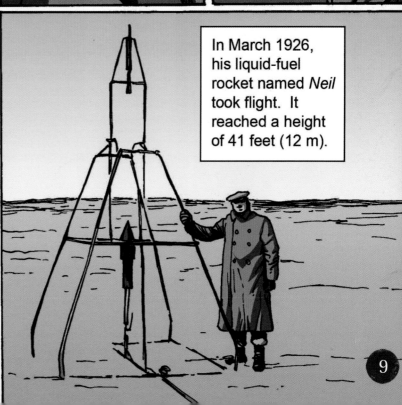

In March 1926, his liquid-fuel rocket named *Neil* took flight. It reached a height of 41 feet (12 m).

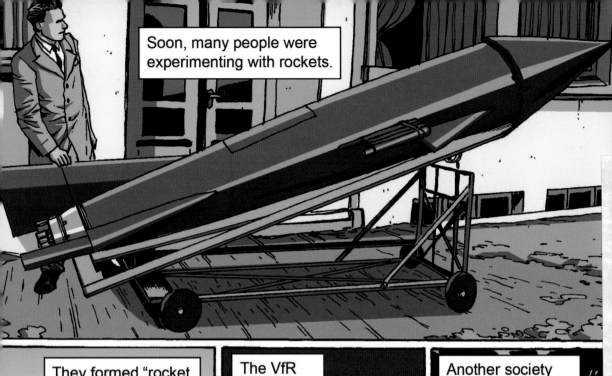

Soon, many people were experimenting with rockets.

They formed "rocket societies."

Engineers and physicists would gather to develop new types of rockets at these societies.

The VfR society was a group from Germany. It launched a liquid-fueled rocket in February 1931.

Another society from the Soviet Union was called GIRD. It launched a hybrid rocket in 1933. The hybrid combined fuel and a chemical to produce thrust.

After a series of experiments, the VfR society developed the A4 rocket. It was larger, traveled farther, and could carry a payload.

This was the first rocket to use a guidance system of gyroscopes.

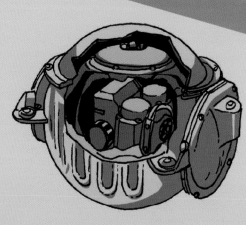

By this time, Adolf Hitler's Nazi Party had taken control of Germany. The Nazis wanted to use the A4 in evil ways.

WORLD WAR II

The world was changing. In 1939, Nazi Germany invaded Poland. This started World War II.

Rockets weren't used at the beginning of the war. But when the Allies invaded later in the war, rockets were turned into weapons. The German A4 was renamed the V2 and was used against Great Britain.

The V2s were not very accurate, so they were aimed at large cities.

Over 3,000 attacks were made with these weapons. Fortunately, the Allies drove the Germans back, so the target cities were out of range.

At the end of the war, the United States and the Soviet Union saw the advances in rocket development that the Germans had made.

Both countries then began to gather all of the information they could about the V2. They even spoke to the scientists working on the V2 program.

Because of Von Braun's work with the Nazis, people were suspicious of him. This made work extremely slow.

One of the people who went to the United States was Wernher Von Braun. He and his team of scientists began the US Space Program.

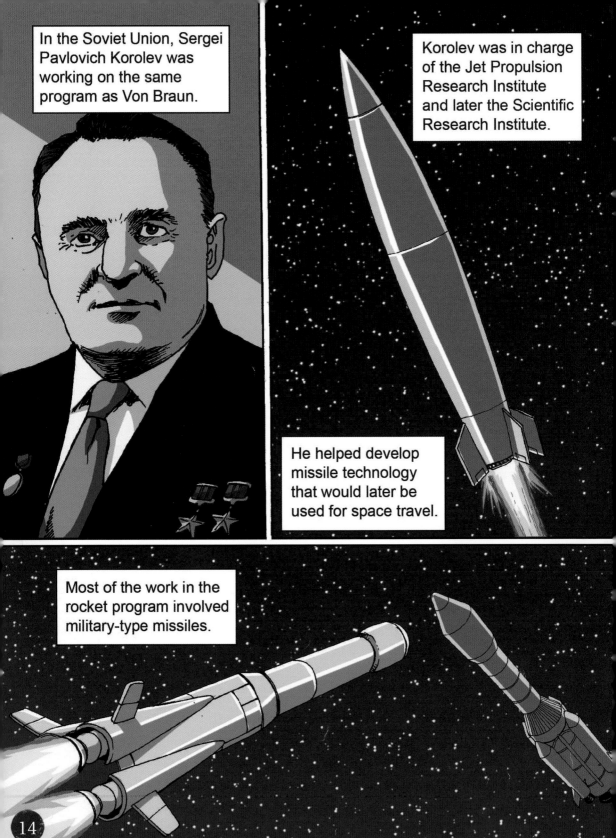

In the Soviet Union, Sergei Pavlovich Korolev was working on the same program as Von Braun.

Korolev was in charge of the Jet Propulsion Research Institute and later the Scientific Research Institute.

He helped develop missile technology that would later be used for space travel.

Most of the work in the rocket program involved military-type missiles.

14

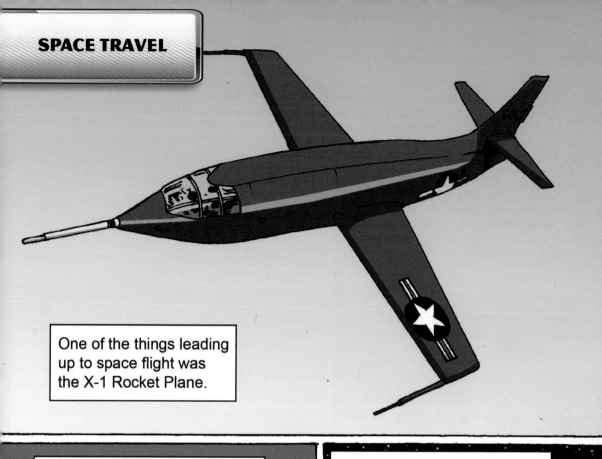

One of the things leading up to space flight was the X-1 Rocket Plane.

Chuck Yeager piloted the X-1 when it became the first aircraft to break the sound barrier.

At the time, space exploration was important to the United States. Meanwhile, the Soviet Union gave the Soviet space program its full support.

Soon, the Soviet Union began testing rockets for a launch into space.

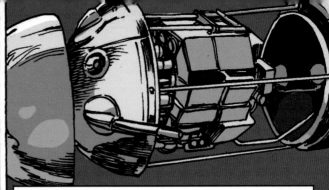

The setbacks did not slow their progress. The Soviets developed a satellite that had temperature and pressure sensors built in.

On October 4, 1957, an R-7 rocket carrying the satellite lifted off from a launchpad in Tyuratam, Russia.

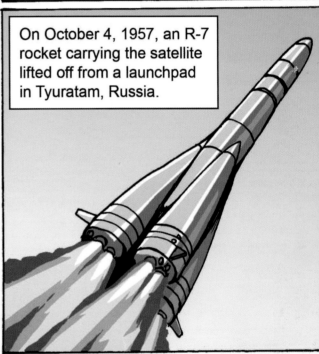

Many problems were found. One test ended in an explosion 100 seconds into the flight.

The mission was a success! *Sputnik 1* successfully orbited Earth, and the Space Age had officially begun.

The United States was surprised by the launch of *Sputnik 1*.

President Dwight D. Eisenhower called for a quick launch of an American satellite.

On December 6, 1958, the United States prepared to launch the Vanguard TV-3 at Cape Canaveral, Florida.

The launch was a failure. It rose to about four feet (1 m) before a huge explosion destroyed the rocket.

With the success of *Sputnik 1*, the space agency was told to continue showing Soviet scientific superiority. Korolev gathered his team of scientists to begin construction of a new satellite.

And to make the flight even more spectacular, it would have a passenger—me!

TEST DOGS

Early in the Soviet space program, dogs were used to help test the rockets.

The Soviets had successfully launched dogs as high as 60 miles (97 km) into the atmosphere.

Many of them returned to Earth unharmed.

The early missions tested equipment and life support systems.

With only a few weeks to accomplish their mission, Korolev's team worked hard to create a capsule. Many things had to be considered.

First, the capsule had to be pressurized and provide oxygen for breathing properly. It also had to remove any carbon dioxide buildup.

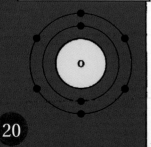

Next, it had to be protected from the radiation of the sun.

And finally, it had to maintain a constant temperature.

NOW WE'RE GETTING TO THE IMPORTANT STUFF-- THE DOGS!

When the capsule was ready, special food and water dispensers were added.

A special waste disposal system was added for the weightless conditions.

Soon, the capsule was complete.

FINALLY, I GET TO TELL YOU ALL ABOUT ME!

I WAS A STRAY ON THE STREETS OF MOSCOW, RUSSIA.

The Soviets thought that stray dogs could better handle the extreme temperatures that were likely during the mission. I was one of ten dogs considered for the flight.

Since I was a stray, no one knows exactly what kind of dog I was. I was definitely not a purebred. Scholars believe I was part terrier and part husky.

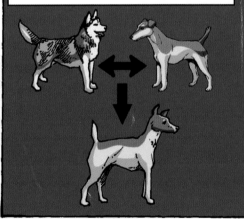

After some training, I was picked to take the flight. They liked my even temper and the light color of my fur, which meant the capsule's cameras could easily see me.

That's when my real training began.

I was placed in a machine called a centrifuge. It simulated the rocket launch.

I was even given special food that I would be eating during my flight.

I was kept in a series of cages that got smaller and smaller. This helped me get used to the small size of the capsule.

23

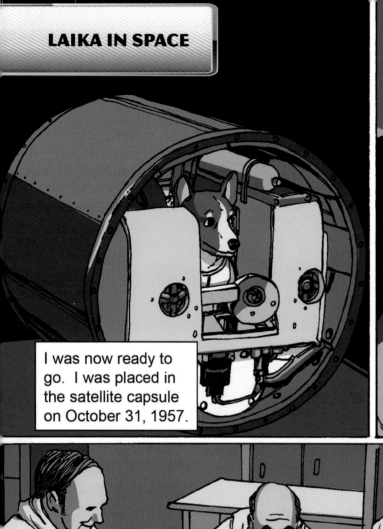

I was now ready to go. I was placed in the satellite capsule on October 31, 1957.

I was watched very carefully over the next few days.

Sensors were placed all over my body to monitor my heart and other bodily functions.

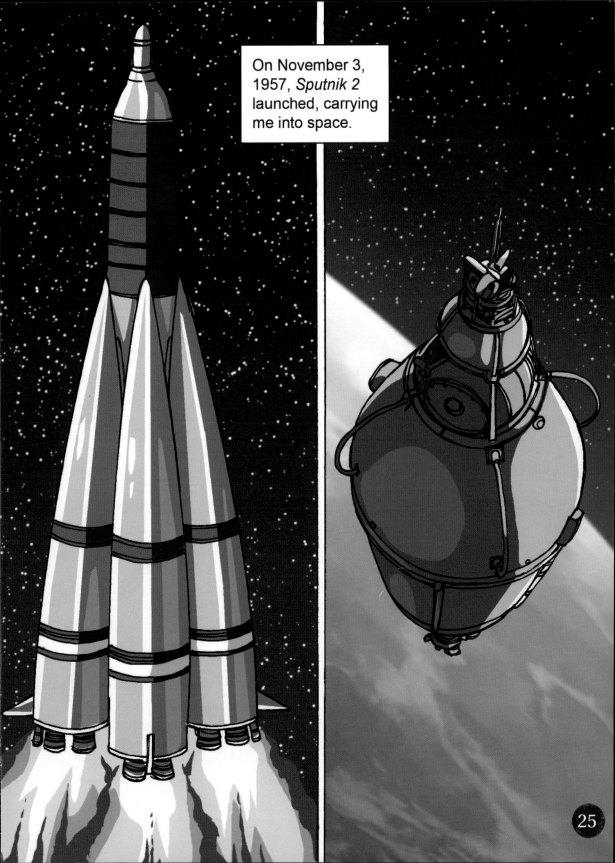

On November 3, 1957, *Sputnik 2* launched, carrying me into space.

I soon settled into orbit, becoming the first animal to travel in space.

The mission did not go smoothly. The core stage of the rocket remained attached to the satellite.

What happened to me next remains something of a mystery.

It was reported at the time that I adjusted to the flight well after some early stress.

Back then, many believed that the Soviet Union could not accomplish this feat. Some even believed *Sputnik 1* was a fake. But *Sputnik 2* was large enough to be seen streaking across the night sky.

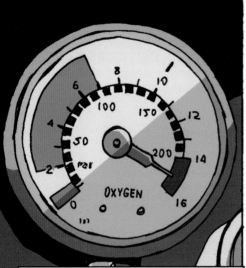

The space agency knew that it would be impossible to get the capsule back. The scientists planned to put me to sleep with some poisoned food before the oxygen ran out.

After November 7, the capsule had radio failure and no readings could be received. It was assumed that I'd passed on about one week into the flight.

The *Sputnik 2* reentered Earth's atmosphere on April 14, 1958. It had been in orbit for 162 days.

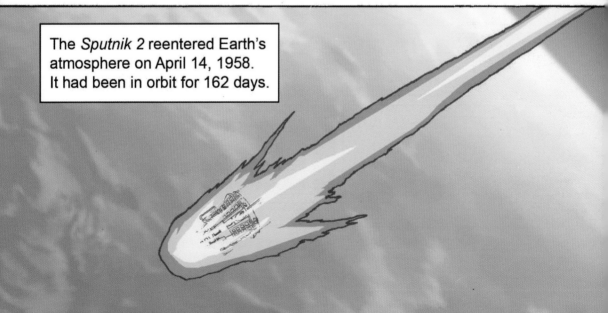

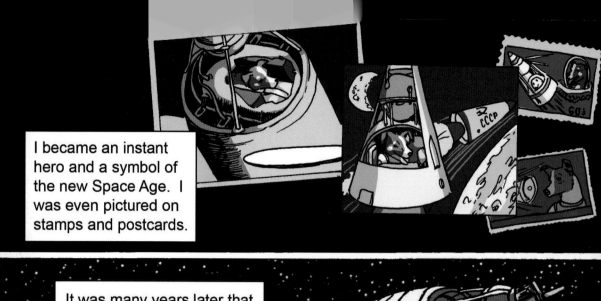

I became an instant hero and a symbol of the new Space Age. I was even pictured on stamps and postcards.

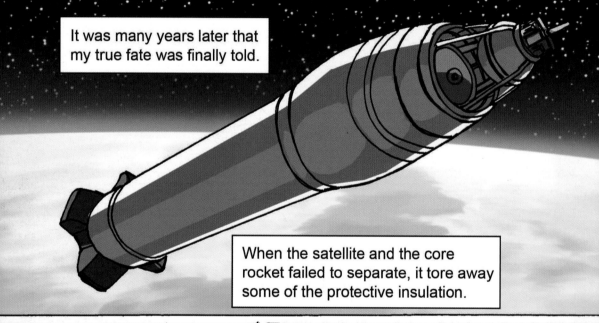

It was many years later that my true fate was finally told.

When the satellite and the core rocket failed to separate, it tore away some of the protective insulation.

This caused the temperature in the capsule to rise to 104 degrees Fahrenheit (40°C).

I mostly likely passed on six to seven hours into the flight from a combination of the heat and flight stress.

I was one of the few animals that died in the space program for both the Soviet Union and United States. I was the only animal to be sent into space with no hope of returning home.

Many believe that scientists could have made a reentry capsule that could have saved me if they had had a little more time. However, the launch was a success. It gave useful information and led the way for human spaceflight and eventually landing on the moon.

I'm so glad I could tell you this story about me and about how I became famous!

29

LAIKA FACTS

Name: Laika
First given name: Kudryavka ("Little Curly")
Nicknames: Zhuchka ("Little Bug"),
    Limonchik ("Lemon"), and Muttnik
Age: About 3 years old
Weight: 13 pounds (6 kg)
Breed: Mongrel stray, believed to be part husky and part terrier

Launch date: November 3, 1957
Launch site: Baikonur Cosmodrome, now located in Kazakhstan
Orbit speed: 18,000 miles per hour (30,000 km/h)

Result: Sensors monitored Laika's heartbeat, blood pressure, and other bodily functions to better understand the physical changes that might happen in space. Her flight proved space travel was possible, and she is remembered as a hero.

Making
1957
History

WEB SITES

To learn more about Laika, visit ABDO Group online at **www.abdopublishing.com**. Web sites about Laika are featured on our Book Links page. These links are routinely monitored and updated to provide the most current information available.

GLOSSARY

allies – people or countries that agree to help each other in times of need. During World War II Great Britain, France, the United States, and the Soviet Union were called the Allies.

atmosphere – the layer of air surrounding Earth.

capsule – a small compartment in a vehicle that is pressurized for space flight.

carbon dioxide – a heavy, fireproof, colorless gas that is burned when fuel containing the element carbon is burned.

centrifuge – a machine using the force one feels when moving away from a curved path. A centrifuge imitates what it is like to move against gravity and is used in training for space travel.

dispenser – a container or a device that feeds specific amounts of something.

gravity – the force that pulls a smaller object toward a larger object.

guidance system – a group of devices used to navigate a ship, rocket, satellite, or other craft.

gyroscope – a device for measuring or maintaining the position of an object.

hybrid – combining two or more functions or ways of operation. For example, gasoline-electric hybrid cars run on both gasoline and electric power.

ignite – to set on fire.

missile – a weapon that is thrown or projected to hit a target.

Nazi – a member of the German political party that controlled Germany under Adolf Hitler.

payload – the people and instruments carried by a vehicle that is needed for its flight.

physicist – a person who studies matter and energy and how they affect each other.

planetary motion – the movement of the planets around the sun.

pressurized – to keep normal air pressure or to put under a greater than normal pressure.

satellite – a manufactured object that orbits Earth. It relays weather and scientific information back to Earth. It also sends television programs across Earth.

sound barrier – a sudden increase of drag that causes an aircraft to slow when it reaches the speed of sound.

superiority – to be better, higher, or greater than something or someone.

suspicious – causing a feeling that something is wrong.

thrust – a force from a jet or a rocket engine that moves the vehicle forward.

INDEX